A

TRIBUTE

TO THE MEMORY OF

HON. WILLIAM L. LEE,

LATE CHIEF JUSTICE OF THE HAWAIIAN KINGDOM,

BY

REV. S. C. DAMON.

PUBLISHED BY REQUEST.

HONOLULU:
H. M. WHITNEY'S PRESS.
1857.

The following discourse was delivered at the Seamen's Chapel in Honolulu, Sabbath evening, May 31, 1857. The funeral exercises were held on the afternoon of the same day, at 4 o'clock, at the large Stone Church, and were numerously attended by both foreigners and natives, including His Majesty, the principal officers of government and members of the Bar. In accordance with the express wishes of the deceased there was no display. The services were conducted in both English and Hawaiian. At the conclusion of the exercises, the procession quietly marched to the Royal Tomb, where the coffin was deposited to await its removal to the United States.

DISCOURSE.

PERHAPS I owe an apology to this audience for permitting the announcement to be made that I would deliver a discourse this evening upon the death of the Chief Justice of this kingdom. Some may have thought it would have been more becoming to have retired from the scenes which we have witnessed, and have spent the closing hours of the Sabbath in silent meditation upon this sad event. To others it may have appeared highly proper and becoming that a voice should be heard from the pulpit, admonishing the people to heed the solemn warning. To have offered protracted remarks, in English, at the church where the funeral exercises were held, when those remarks would have been unintelligible to the majority present, would have seemed quite improper; hence you have been invited to assemble this evening in this chapel, where the deceased was accustomed to worship during the period of his residence upon the islands. As we shall no more meet with him here to worship God, how becoming that we devoutly contemplate the event of his removal from our midst to the scenes of another world, and profit by briefly reviewing his public and private life, which for the last ten years has been passing before us.

I have selected a passage from the prophecy of Amos, thinking it not altogether inappropriate on this occasion, as the theme of discourse:

"THUS SAITH THE LORD: FOR THREE TRANSGRESSIONS OF MOAB, AND FOR FOUR * * * I WILL CUT OFF THE JUDGE FROM THE MIDST THEREOF."—2: 1, 3.

It should be carefully borne in mind that God would not cut off the judge and inflict other calamities upon the Moabites, (for it was to the nation of Moab that this language refers) because he had failed to perform his duty, but because the people had failed in their duty. "Thus saith the Lord; for three transgressions of Moab, and for four * * I will cut off the judge from the midst thereof." I would not assert that God has removed the Chief Justice of this kingdom because of the people's transgressions—but I am prepared to declare that his life has been shortened, and death hastened through his intense desire and unwearied efforts to administer justice among this transgressing people. We are all able to bear witness to his anxious solicitude, lest this people should be cut off in their transgressions.

1. I would remark, in the first place, *that the bestowal of an upright, able and honorable Judge is one of the greatest blessings which God grants to any people.* An inspired writer has recorded, "For there is no power but of God; the powers that be are ordained of God." These "powers that be" refer to human governments, and among nations most advanced in civilization, these powers have come to be distributed under the general terms, *Legislative*, *Judicial* and *Executive.* I will not linger to make remarks defining the nature, or showing the importance of maintaining harmony among these separate powers, or efficiency in their operation, but proceed to state that words would fail to express, in too strong language, the value and importance of securing honesty, integrity, dignity and efficiency in the judiciary department. If there be weakness or corruption in this department, the whole fabric of human government would fail of accomplishing its full intent; hence the truth of the proposition which I have just uttered; viz., "that the bestowal of an upright, able and honorable judge is one of the greatest blessings which God grants to any people." You will, of course, understand me as referring to blessings of a temporal nature.

I now feel prepared to show, that considering the peculiar circumstances of this nation when Mr. Lee was invited to preside over its judiciary department, and the eminent abilities which he has evinced as a Judge, his life and services have been an invaluable blessing to the Hawaiian nation. But what were some of the peculiar circumstances of this nation at the period of his appointment? Ten years ago, scarcely were the first principles of order and regularity in the courts of this kingdom defined and established. This will appear, when I refer to a Reference, or Court of Appeal, which was holding its sessions in this very building, on the very day, the 12th of October, 1846, when Mr. Lee landed in Honolulu. On the morning of that day I visited the brig *Henry*, just arrived after a long and tempestuous passage of eight months from the United States. I was then introduced to Mr. Lee, as a young lawyer on his way to Oregon, there to commence the practice of his profession. After calling at my house, I invited him to visit the Bethel Vestry, where was then in progress a trial of marked character in the history of this nation. By persons acquainted with that event, it may readily be imagined what must have been some of the reflections of his mind upon that occasion, trained in the severe school, and under the eminent teachings of Judge Story and Professor Greenleaf, of Harvard University Law School. Verily he must have seen and felt the need of some able jurist and legal adviser to give shape and order to the Courts of the Hawaiian

Kingdom. Such was the unsettled state of affairs in those days in this nation, that the language of Isaiah might not inappropriately have been applied: "And judgment is turned away backward, and justice standeth afar off; for truth is fallen in the street, and equity cannot enter. Yea, truth faileth, and he that departeth from evil maketh himself a prey, and the Lord saw it, that there was no judgment." 59 : 14, 15. Some, if not all the departments of government, were then in an unsettled state. It was a critical period. The old order of public affairs was passing away. A transition-state was existing, and the result was quite uncertain. It is not intended by these remarks to cast the least reflection upon those who had been laboring to build up a temple of justice upon the ruins of the old feudal laws, arbitrary rule and system of *tabus*, which had existed, and the influence of which was still felt. Messrs. Richards, Judd, Wyllie, Ricord and others had labored long and arduously at the work. They were called to overcome prejudices, and alter usages cemented by antiquity, strengthened by selfishness, and consolidated by the inherent love of power, which reigns in the human breast. At a glance, it will appear that some master-mind was imperatively required to bring order out of confusion. That mind needed to be eminently well-trained and well-balanced. The materials to be moulded and fashioned into order required no wild theorist of the French School of '93 or '48; no political aspirant or ambitious demagogue—but a cool, careful, thoughtful, practical, conservative, well-trained, self-reliant and Christian mind. Already had Mr. Richards made a pilgrimage to the United States in the year 1837, partly for the purpose of securing a person possessing such a mind. He failed in that object, and on returning, by invitation of the King and Chiefs, undertook the arduous work himself. The results of his laborious efforts, amid difficulties great and embarrassing were the Constitution and Code of 1840. Men of eminent legal abilities have pronounced these as worthy of great praise, considering the circumstances of their production—but they were not adapted to the advancing state of affairs in the Hawaiian kingdom. The time had come for an entire remodeling. This was commenced by Mr. Ricord, but more fully carried out by him, whose earthly remains we have this day committed to the Royal Tomb of the Hawaiian kings.

I am now prepared to declare, that such have been the traits and qualities manifested in the life and conduct of Judge Lee, that he was just the man required for the station which he has filled with so much honor and credit to himself, and with so much usefulness and benefit to this nation. His excellent natural abilities, the peculiar constitution of his mind, so clear, searching and discriminative—the inherent truthfulness and uprightness of his character, joined to an education, thorough and practical, all combined, rendered him eminently fitted for the work he had to do—and he performed it as no other man in this part of the world could have done.

By his early associate, fellow-voyager, and bosom friend, Mr. C. R. Bishop, I have been kindly furnished with the following sketch of Mr. Lee's early life:

"Mr. Lee was born in Sandy Hill, Washington County, New York, February 25th, 1821. At the age of thirteen he entered the Norwich University in the State of Vermont, where he remained two years, at the end of which time he left the institution and engaged in the business of Civil Engineering in the service of his native State. In this profession he rose so rapidly, that at the end of three years he left it, filling the post of Resident Engineer. He then returned to Norwich University, where be graduated at the age of twenty, taking the first honors.

"After leaving the University he received the appointment of Superintendant at the Military Academy at Portsmouth, Virginia, in which situation he remained a year. Having decided upon adopting the law as his profession, he now entered Harvard University where he finished the course of law studies, under those eminent jurists, Judge Story and Professor Greenleaf. Just as he was about establishing himself in the practice of his profession he was attacked with a violent hemorrhage of the lungs, and his case was considered for some months a hopeless one, but a naturally strong constitution triumphed over the disease, and in the year 1844 he was able to commence the practice of the law in the City of Troy, New York. Here he remained till the recurrence of pulmonary symptoms warned him that he must seek a warmer climate. At that time public attention was strongly directed towards the new territory of Oregon, and it was supposed to offer unusual inducements to settlers on account of the salubrity of its climate, the fertility of its soil, and the prospect of its speedy growth. Deciding to cast his fortunes in that new country, he embarked, with a company of fourteen others, on the brig *Henry*, bound for Columbia River *via* the Sandwich Islands."

Thus it would appear that, for a quarter of a century, God was in His kind providence gradually educating a young man for the responsible station of Chief Justice of this kingdom. I would remark, however, that Mr. Lee had no intention of remaining here on his arrival. The most distant thought probably had not entered his mind that he would spend his days at the Sandwich Island. But God had led him by a way that he knew not.

2. I would remark in the second place, *that the death of an upright, able and honorable Judge is a great calamity; but the calamity is partially mitigated by the consideration that his wise decisions and important services will exert an important influence long after their author may have passed away.* When Sir Mathew Hale, Marshall, Story and other eminent men, who have adorned the Judicial Bench by their great abili-

ties and distinguished talents died, their influence did not cease to be felt. As has been aptly and eloquently remarked by Daniel Webster, "A truly great man, when Heaven vochsafes so rare a gift, is not a temporary flame burning brightly for a while, and then giving place to returning darkness. It is rather a spark of fervent heat, as well as radiant light, with power to enkindle the common mind, so that when it glimmers in its own decay, and finally goes out in death, no night follows, but it leaves the world all light, all on fire from the potent contact of its own spirit."

I do not claim for the deceased, tha the was to be ranked among the greatest lawgivers and judges, whose names adorn ancient or modern history, but I do claim that he was a man of no ordinary ability and judicial knowledge, combined with stern integrity and unflinching rectitude. In the latter qualities especially, he was great, and as such we shall ever love to think of him. In old Testament times no higher qualifications were sought in a judge than that he should fear God, and be no respecter of persons, dispensing justice alike, to the rich and the poor, the powerful and weak. In this respect Judge Lee gained an enviable reputation. He had the fear of God before his mind, and the poor man's appeal was not in vain. While he befriended the poor and weak, he was, by no means, unmindful of the prerogatives of the King and Chiefs. Though not a subject of the Realm, they never found a warmer and more loyal friend, or a safer and more unselfish adviser.* Their rights were sacred in his estimation. Knowing that the tendency of his mind was truly democratic or republican, I have watched, with no little interest, the important services which he was enabled to render to His Majesty, now upon the throne, and to his predecessor. Many of the most important questions which have come before the rulers of this nation, and called from them prompt and ready action, have been decided upon his opinion, for when that was known nothing more was said. Judge Lee's opinion having been ascertained, the difficult point was considered as decided. Such confidence is a plant of slow growth, but its blossoms are beautiful and its fruit excellent. Long will he be remembered as a member of the King's Privy Council, and Chief Justice of the Hawaiian kingdom. As has been truthfully remarked: "Wherever the Sandwich Islands are known, Mr. Lee has been heard of as a pillar of the State, and through his efforts rather than those of any other individual, and the honest tendency of his public acts, the Government has acquired a reputation and prestige which give it strength beyond its proportions. In undertaking to reduce the Judiciary Department to order, and put our courts of law

* By Leters Patent of Denization conferred upon him, when he accepted office, he was not required to take the oath of allegiance.

into a position to command respect, he succeeded well indeed; and the principal tribunal, over which he presided, acquired such a name for wisdom, combined with probity, not to be questioned, that parties often left their cases with the Court as an umpire of their own choice. In one word, on whatever there is of progress, and whatever there is of order observable throughout the length and breadth of this archipelago, it may be said that more or less conspicuously the mark of Mr. Lee's hand is seen. His associates in the public services—and he was, during his career, brought into relations with almost every officer of the Government, from the highest to the lowest—will acknowledge the value they attached to his judgment, the soundness of his reasoning, and the facility he possessed of rapidly unrobing a subject of its difficulties and laying bare its very heart."*

But I should be doing great inujstice to the character of the deceased did I go no farther than invite you to view him as Judge upon the Bench, although occupying that position with dignity and usefulness for so many years. He was a true friend of the people, and his influence extended to the humblest habitation from Hawaii to Kauai. Early upon his arrival, having become most intimately acquainted with the condition of the nation, and understanding the mode of conducting other departments of public service he was always ready to lend a helping hand, and impart the aid of his ever active and vigorous mind. Upon the death of Mr. Richards, he was appointed President of the Land Commission, and in this capacity he performed an immense amount of public service.† Some of the results of those labors are set forth in the following paragraphs, copied from his first address, in 1852, before the Royal Hawaiian Agricultural Society. I shall never forget with what animation and fervency he uttered them standing in this desk. In referring to the inestimable boon conferred upon the nation, in allowing the common people to become proprietors of the soil, he remarked:

"I thank God, that these things are at an end, and that the poor kanaka may now stand upon the border of his kalo patch, and holding his fee simple patent in his hand, bid defiance to the world! Yes, I thank God that he has moved the hearts of the King and Chiefs of these Islands to let the oppressed go free! The granting of Royal Patents in fee simple to the common people for their lands, is the brightest jewel that adorns the crown of Kamehameha III., and will shine with increasing lustre long after his body shall have mouldered to its mother earth!"

And in the closing paragraphs of the same address he adds: "Must they

* "Polynesian," May 30.

† In justice to the character of Judge Lee, it should be stated that, although he performed a great amount of labor in the Land Commission, and other departments of the public service, yet he never received extra compensation.

die! Will we let them die without making one struggle to save them from the grave to which they are hastening! No, my friends, justice and humanity forbid! Let us not forget that the soil, whose treasures we would unlock, was once the undisputed heritage of the poor Hawaiian; and let us remember too, that though the white man bore the glad tidings of salvation to his wondering ear, he planted in his veins the disease from which the great reaper Death has gathered full many a harvest. Though but a lone remnant remains, let us strive to gird it with strength to wrestle with its approaching destiny—to arm it with the healthy body and vigorous frame, the only weapons that can stay the hand of the Destroyer. Then if our efforts to send a quickening life pulse through the heart of this wasting nation avail not, we can but commend it to Him in whose hands are the issues of life and death—to Him who counteth the nations as the small dust of the balance, and who taketh up the isles as a very little thing."

It was in this capacity, as President of the Land Commission, more than in any other that the physical and mental powers of his naturally strong constitution were overtasked. These efforts, in addition to what he was already performing, made the weight of his public service well nigh crushing, and yet so long as there was a claim unsettled, he was at his post of duty. It never can be told how anxiously he toiled in this business, and if it were told, the world could not appreciate the statement. There were others too who labored with him in this arduous undertaking.

While engaged as a Judge and President of the Land Commission, there came in 1853, that terrible malady, the small pox. By many it will be remembered how diligently, arduously and tenderly he labored for this afflicted people. Daily did he visit the habitations where more than seventy persons were lying sick with this terrible disease. It was at this critical period that his old pulmonary difficulties re-appeared, and their ravages ceased not until death closed his earthly career.

A paragraph from the *Polynesian* of May 30, 1857, will still further unfold the amount of public service which he performed for the nation:

"From the time of Mr. Lee's arrival here until he became too ill to take an active part in the transactions of public business, he was a laborious member of the Privy Council, where his honesty of purpose, independence of character and sound judgment, justly gained him great weight and influence. When, in 1855, he resolved to visit the United States for the benefit of his health, his Majesty appointed him Envoy Extraordinary and Minister Plenipotentiary to Washington, in which capacity he negotiated with the Cabinet of President Pierce a treaty of commercial reciprocity, which was calculated to have given a great impulse to our agriculture and commerce had it been sanctioned by the Senate of the United States.

"Mr. Lee was Speaker in the House of Representatives during the session of 1851, at the close of which he was appointed as one of three Commissioners charged with the duty of framing a new Constitution, the original draft of which was prepared by him for submission to the King and the Legislative Body. The Penal Code, and many of the most important laws to be found upon our statute books subsequent to the year 1847, were drawn up by him; and he was one of three Commissioners appointed in 1856 to revise the existing laws, and prepare an entire Civil Code. During last summer, while the guest of the Hon. R. Moffit, at Kahuku, Judge Lee, with the assistance of Judge Robertson, was engaged upon the last named work, which, on account of his subsequent severe illness, still remains unfinished.

"Up to the time of his visit to the United States he had, in addition to his other duties, to maintain an extensive correspondence with persons, both foreigners and natives, resident in other parts of the kingdom; with the latter he corresponded in their own language, in which, amidst all his cares, he succeeded in acquiring a fair degree of proficiency."

Mr. Lee took a lively interest in all the benevolent societies and associations of the day. In July, 1847, he was elected President of the "Oahu Temperance Society," and on the opening of the following year delivered an address before the Society, (now nearly out of print) replete with sound sentiment, eloquent paragraphs, and breathing a purity of moral feeling and fervency of benevolent emotion, which indicated a heart glowing with the liveliest sympathy towards his fellow men. The following are the closing sentences of that address:

"The New Year, my friends, has come to remind us that our time for doing good, and days for usefulness are shortening. Time rolls us onward, and onward, and as we *must* go onward, let our motto be "ONWARD AND UPWARD." Let us ponder on the past, and improve on the present! To-morrow may not be ours to improve! Death is all around us, and how soon he may rap at our door, God only knows! Not a word do I utter, not a breath do I breathe, but some spirit takes its flight to the boundless regions of eternity. The earth is still fresh upon the grave of one of our number, and how many cheeks, now blooming with the rosy hue of life and health, will be blanched by the cold hand of death before another year rolls round, is not for us to know. How many, or who will fall beneath the dreadful stroke, is not for us to know; but it is for us to know, that we are liable to death at any moment. I repeat it then, let us improve the present—let us make the most of it—let us daily improve in temperance, knowledge, industry and virtue. Let us so live that death, come when it may, we can meet it with a smile, and look calmly back upon life with the satisfaction that we have not lived to curse, but bless mankind. Go on my brethren, in the good work you have commenced! Go on in constant and ardent labor! and however small the perceptible results of that labor, you will at least have the joy of an approving conscience, and the smiles of heaven upon your well meant endeavors! Go on, go on! and may the new year to come be a *happy* new year, bringing us the glad tidings of mental, moral, and physical improvement!"

He was successively elected President of the Royal Hawaiian Agricultural Society, from 1852 to 1856, when his absence from the Islands and state of health rendered it absolutely impossible for him to serve longer in that capacity.

In 1854 he was elected President of the Hawaiian Bible Society, and in 1856, a member of the Board of the Trustees of Oahu College. In no sphere of active benevolent effort, was he more interested than in the establishment of the Honolulu Sailors' Home. At the time of his death he was Vice President of the Society, the office of President being held by His Majesty. He presided at the meetings of the Board, and often acted upon committees, but in whatever capacity called to act, he manifested a willingness to discharge his duty, and an aptitude for business, rendering it exceedingly pleasant to labor with him. Long will he be remembered by his fellow trustees in this capacity.

I have hitherto spoken of Judge Lee as a public man, and as called upon to discharge duties and fill offices of trust connected with this kingdom, and the foreign community. It remains for me that I briefly refer to him as a private individual. It has been truthfully and aptly remarked that every public man has two sides to his character, viz.: that which is public, and that which is private. Between the two there is not unfrequently a sad discrepancy. The one may appear comparatively bright, while the other is very dark. Not so, however, with the subject of our present remarks. There was a beautiful harmony and correspondence between his public and private character. For a public man he was the most accessible man I ever knew. Not only was his advice ready and prompt upon matters of weighty import, but he was ready on all suitable occasions to sit down, consult with and advise the humblest of His Majesty's subjects in regard to their most trivial *pilikias*. I do not believe the person is to be found among either foreigners or natives who was denied a hearing, or was rudely thrust away. Never did the sentiment of Terence, the old Roman poet, apply to any public man more aptly than it did to him: "I am a man, and think nothing concerning mankind foreign from my own concern." As a kind neighbor and friend, few persons possessed as many amiable qualities or desirable traits of character. He was beloved by all, but, by some, most enthusiastically, and the bonds of friendship drew firmer and closer as the period approached when he must be separated from them.

The present is not the time or place to draw aside the veil and expose to view the feelings of the heart now widowed and desolate, or expatiate upon the sundering of the dearest and holiest of all earthly ties of relationship; but our fervent prayer is, that the Gracious Being in whom he trusted, may comfort the bereaved and afflicted one in this day and hour of her anguish and sorrow.

It remains, however, before closing my remarks, to make an allusion to one other view of his character. When a man departs who has occupied a large share of public attention, moved in spheres of influence, and occupied stations of great official trust and responsibility, there is a deep solicitude, in many minds, to learn what were his views upon religious subjects, or did he believe in the principles of Christianity as revealed in the Bible. Upon this topic, I feel prepared to speak with freedom, and in language which will admit of no doubtful interpretation. Judge Lee died, as he lived, not only a theoretical, but a practical believer in the Christian religion. He was a doer, as well as hearer, of the word. During the last few months of his life he expressed himself with a freedom which leaves no possible doubt upon the minds of his friends, that he embraced the Gospel of our Lord and Savior Jesus Christ, and relied solely upon the merits of the Redeemer as the ground of his acceptance, when he should be called to appear before his final Judge. He was no sectarian. He did not trouble his mind about what he styled "the dry bones of creeds and theological systems," but looked directly to Christ and Him crucified as his only hope of salvation. He remarked to me, not long since, that perhaps his views approached nearer those of the Methodist Episcopal Church than those of any other denomination, although he could not hold to all their doctrines. That was the belief of his father. In that he was educated.

Two weeks ago to-day, it was my privilege to officiate, as a minister of the Gospel, in a capacity, the remembrance of which is most comforting and refreshing. At his request I administered to him the rite of Baptism, after which, in company with a few Christian friends, he partook of, for the first and last time, the precious memorials of our Saviour's body and blood. That was a season which will long be remembered by those assembled in that "upper chamber."

"The chamber where the good man meets his fate,
Is privileged beyond the common walk
Of virtuous life, *quite on the verge of Heaven.*"

During his long sickness, his mind, naturally cheerful and buoyant, has been preserved in a peculiarly happy frame. I would state in this connection, that, although he had not made previously a public profession of religion by uniting with a Christian church, yet for many years he had indulged the hope of a Christian, and led a life of prayer. Here was the grand secret of his undeviating perseverance in so many laudable undertakings. He often expressed regrets in his last days that he had not more publicly made known his religious views; and, on one occasion, remarked that his greatest desire to live was, that he might set a better Christian example, and do more for Christ. He was eminently charitable in his feelings towards all, to whatever denomination they might belong. Among the last words which I ever heard fall from his lips were, "*Be charitable. There are Christians in all denominations! Be charitable!*" I hope that I may profit by this injunction, for I doubt not if he could address us from the eternal world, his language would still be, "Be charitable."

Having thus recapitulated the leading events in his life, and reviewed his public and private career, surely we have abundant occasion to mourn the loss of so valuable a man, cut off in the midst of his days and in the vigor of manhood.

> "It matters little at what hour of the day
> The righteous falls asleep. Death cannot come
> To him untimely who is fit to die;
> The less of this cold world, the more of Heaven—
> The briefer life, the earlier immortality."

Never has one been called from this community, in view of whose death all classes have so much occasion to drop a tear of sorrow at his tomb. But our loss, we hope, is his infinite and eternal gain.

APPENDIX.

[FROM THE PACIFIC COMMERCIAL ADVERTISER OF JUNE 11.]

THE death of the Hon. William L. Lee, Chief Justice of the Supreme Court, and Chancellor of the Kingdom, though not unexpected, has spread an unusual gloom over our community. His many admirable qualities of mind and heart, so rarely combined in one individual, had won for him the esteem and confidence of all classes, both among natives and foreigners, while his eminent public services have rendered his death a heavy national calamity.

The universal sorrow everywhere manifested for his loss, the thousands who gathered to pay the last sad tribute to his memory, the crowded churches where his life, his services and his virtues were made the theme of discourse, are evidences of the deep affection with which he had inspired the people among whom the best years of his life have been spent. In him the King has lost a faithful and judicious Counsellor, the Bench a wise and upright Judge, the foreign community a warm and liberal friend, and the nation a benefactor, whose best energies were devoted to its welfare, and whose life was worn out by his unremitting labors in its service. In the appropriate language of our cotemporary of the *Polynesian*, "wherever the Sandwich Islands are known, Mr. Lee has been heard of as a pillar of the State, and through his efforts, rather than those of any other individual, and the honest tendency of his public acts, the government has acquired a reputation and prestige which give it a strength beyond its proportions. In one word, on whatever there is of progress and whatever there is observable throughout the length and breadth of this archipelago, it may be said that more or less conspicuously the mark of Mr. Lee's hand is seen."

Mr. Lee was born at Sandy Hill, Washington County, in the State of New York, on the 25th of February, 1821. At the age of thirteen he entered the Norwich University in the State of Vermont, where he remained two years, at the end of which time he left the institution and engaged in the business of a Civil Engineer in the service of his native State. In this profession he rose so rapidly that at the end of only three years he left it, having already filled the post of Resident Engineer. He next returned to Norwich University, where he graduated at the age of twenty, taking the first honors. On leaving the University he received the appointment of Superintendent of the Military Academy at Portsmouth, Virginia, in which position he remained one year. Having at this time of his maturity decided upon adopting the law as his profession, he entered the Law School at Harvard University, where he remained till he had completed the course of study under those eminent jurists, Judge Story and Professor Greenleaf. It is no small praise to say that he was honored with the confidence and friendship of both these distinguished men. Judge Story furnished him with letters of reference when he left the Law School, and with Professor Greenleaf he was in constant correspondence until his death.

When Mr. Lee was about to establish himself as a practitioner, he was attacked with a violent hemorrhage of the lungs, and his case was, for some months, considered to be a hopeless one—but a naturally strong constitution triumphed over the disease, and in the year 1844 he was able to commence the practice of law in the city of Troy, New York. Here he applied himself to his profession with the unremitting industry which characterised him, until his labors brought on a recurrence of pulmonary symptoms, which warned him to seek a more genial climate. At this time public attention was strongly directed towards the new Territory of Oregon, which was supposed to offer unusual advantages to settlers, as well in the salubrity of its climate as the fertility of its soil, and its prospect of a speedy growth. Deciding then to cast his fortunes in that young country, Mr. Lee embarked, with a company of fourteen others on board the brig *Henry*, bound for Columbia River by way of the Sandwich Islands, and, after a tempestuous voyage of about eight months, the vessel arrived at Honolulu on the 12th of October, 1846, to the surprise of many who had given her up as lost.

Mr. Lee had not entertained the most distant idea of remaining at these Islands. The time of his arrival, however, and the long delay of the vessel here, caused by the extensive repairs which were found necessary, seemed providential. It was a critical period in the affairs of this young nation. The Government was engaged in a controversy with some of the foreign residents, which had embroiled nearly the whole of the community, and which menaced its very existence. The bitter and angry feelings which had grown up among the partisans on either side, had almost caused open rupture. General uneasiness and distrust prevailed. The course of Attorney-General Ricord, the only officer of the Government of legal education and profession, was ill-calculated to conciliate the contending parties, or to inspire that confidence in the Government which was so necessary to its peace and prosperity. The laws drawn up by him were ambiguous and complicated, and the tribunals of the realm were looked upon by a large and intelligent class of the community, rather as instruments of oppression than sources of redress from injustice.

At this epoch, the advent of an upright, able and impartial Judge, to whom all parties could look with confidence, seemed the only event that could restore order out of chaos, and save the country and the Government from utter confusion. But in those days of isolation, and almost non-intercourse with civilised countries, this seemed too great a boon to expect. It was at this period that Mr. Lee accidently arrived here, and subsequent events soon showed him to be the very man for the emergency. It was fortunate for the nation when he accepted the post of Presiding Judge offered him by the late King. Mr. Lee was not easily induced to change his design, and though the King, thinking that the oath of allegiance, which had been required of other government officers, might be objectionable, offered to confer on him Letters Patent of denization, by which he acquired all the rights of an Hawaiian subject, without forfeiting those of an American citizen, yet it was with reluctance that he consented to remain, in what then seemed doubtless a narrow sphere of action, compared with the mighty West. But, from the day of his accepting office under this Government until that of his death, he served it with a zeal, industry, ability and success, of which history affords but few examples.

It is impossible, within the limits of a newspaper article, to do more than allude to some of the eminent services of this extraordinary man; but however arduous were the duties of his own particular department, and they were never neglected or slighted, yet, whenever any of the wheels of government were stopped or impeded, his shoulder was ever ready for the emergency, and never was it applied in vain. To quote again from our cotemporary, "In undertaking to reduce the Judiciary Department to order, and put our Courts of Law into a position to command respect, he succeeded well indeed; and the principal tribunal, over which he presided, acquired such a name for wisdom, combined with probity not to be questioned, that parties often left their cases with the Court as an umpire of their own choice."

As President of the Board of Commissioners, he performed a responsible and arduous labor. As one of the Commissioners charged with the duty of framing a new Constitution, he prepared the original draft—a task of no little magnitude, when we consider the incongruous elements to be united and reconciled in its formation. The Penal Code and many of the most important laws were drawn up by him. As one of the Commissioners to prepare a new Civil Code, he taxed his waning strength in his labors with Judge Robertson on this work, which his death has left unfinished. As Envoy Extraordinary and Minister Plenipotentiary to Washington, he negotiated a Treaty of Reciprocity, which, if ever confirmed by the United States Senate, will confer great benefits on this kingdom. For all these extra labors, arduous as they were, to which he devoted the hours of day and night which most men consider necessary for relaxation and repose, and under which his own health gave way, he steadily and repeatedly refused any additional compensation. The Privy Council and the Legislature have in vain endeavored to force on him some remuneration for his many voluntary and severe labors; but his reply was that his salary as Judge was sufficiently liberal, and that he considered the Government which employed him, entitled to his services in whatever capacity they could be made useful.

Mr. Lee possessed the entire confidence of both the late and the present King; and on more than one occasion has His Majesty, Kamehameha IV., evinced his appreciation of his services and his virtues, his ardent attachment to his person, and his deep solicitude for his recovery.

We have spoken thus far of Mr. Lee as a public man, but a sketch of his character would be incomplete without an allusion to his private and social virtues. As is rarely the case, his public and private characters were in singular and beautiful harmony. No man has ever possessed the entire confidence of so many of all ranks and conditions, both among natives and foreigners, as he did. He was looked up to as the counsellor and guide of many who were very much his seniors in years, and among whom his loss will be deeply felt throughout the group. United to his glowing benevolence and love for his fellow men, he had the happy faculty of appreciating at once the good qualities of those with whom he was brought in contact, and of stimulating their exercises and development. To his more intimate friends he was ardent, warm-hearted and generous. Always ready and anxious to serve them, his eminently unselfish disposition rendered him unwilling to receive any return. To such an extent did he carry this feeling, that though towards the close of his illness, his failing strength and frequently recurring ill-turns rendered it necessary for him to have constant attention, yet he refused to allow any of his friends to watch with him, though they earnestly pleaded for this privilege. And it was not till the very night of his departure that he consented to have any other attendance than that of the faithful and cherished partner of his lot. In 1849 he married Miss Catherine E. Newton, of Albany, New York. In her heavy bereavement words of comfort are of little avail. But it may be some consolation to her to know that she has the heart-felt sympathy of many warm friends, and that her sorrow is in some measure shared by those who found in the departed a friend that sticketh closer than a brother.

Mr. Lee was the founder, and for several years the President of the Royal Hawaiian Agricultural Society, and was indefatigable in his efforts to promote the cause of agriculture. He was one of the most efficient members of the Board of Trustees of the Sailors' Home, the success of which was an object very dear to his heart. He was President of the Hawaiian Bible Society, a strong friend of the temperance cause, and an active and liberal promoter of benevolent or religious objects, to the aid of which he brought the same untiring zeal and energy that he exhibited in his daily avocations. Most implicitly did he follow in everything which he undertook the Scripture injunction, "whatsoever thy hands find to do, do it *with all thy might.*" He was a sincere and humble Christian, and though making no display of his piety, yet the tree was known by its fruit, and his daily walk and conversation bore witness that he had made the Divine Master his pattern. He had not united with any church, not that he hesitated to confess his Saviour before men, but because he had an insuperable objection to the adoption of any creeds, which he looked upon as barriers of human invention, dividing Christians from each other. He bore his severe and protracted sufferings without a murmur, maintaining his characteristic cheerfulness to the last, his only dread being that he should outlive his usefulness, and become a burden to his friends. To one of them who remarked to him that he seemed very happy, he replied, "yes, I *am very happy;* I am gliding peacefully down the stream of life, gathering flowers from either bank as I pass." In such a resigned and happy frame of mind did this eminent man, having "set his house in order," await the expected summons. And though he had reached but half the alloted "three score and ten," yet in that short period he had accomplished a lifetime of usefulness. He has early gone to his reward, but his bright example remains to us. Well will it be for us both as a nation, and as individuals, if we strive to follow it, and to heed the lessons which it teaches.

RESOLUTIONS PASSED BY THE PRIVY COUNCIL, JUNE 1, 1857.

WHEREAS, by the death of the Honorable William L. Lee, late Chief Justice and Chancellor of the Kingdom, this Council has, in obedience to the Divine will, been deprived of the co-operation and counsel of one of its most valuable members, and sustained a loss that must be permanently felt,

Therefore, BE IT RESOLVED, that this Council, having heard of the death of the late Chief Justice Lee with more than ordinary feelings of regret, and considering the loss as one that neither the King nor his Council can hope to repair, when the soundness of his judgment, the perseverance of his business habits and his urbanity of manner are called to mind, hereby express, with a view to its being put upon record, the deep sorrow with which this blow has filled them; and

Further BE IT RESOLVED, That this Council offer to the King their respectful expression of the regret with which they remember the loss which he has personally met by the removal of a Counsellor in whom he has so long reposed confidence, and that with so much cause; and

Further BE IT RESOLVED, That the sincere condolences of this Council be offered to the bereaved widow of the late Chief Justice, whose affliction they can understand upon the removal of a kind and tender husband, whose domestic qualities added not a little to the value of his public services, and

Further BE IT RESOLVED, That the members of this Council wear the usual badge of mourning for thirty days; and

Lastly BE IT RESOLVED, That the Secretary be directed to make these Resolutions of record and forward a copy of the same to the widow of our lamented associate.

By order of the Privy Council, June 1, 1857.

L. ANDREWS, Secretary.

At a meeting of the Bar and Officers of the Court held at the office of A. B. Bates, Esq., upon request of the District Attorney of Oahu, on the occasion of the decease of Hon. W. L. Lee, Mr. Bates was called to the Chair, and Mr. J. E. Barnard requested to act as Secretary, the following members of the Bar and officers of the Court being present:

A. B. Bates, J. Montgomery, J. W. Marsh, J. P. Griswold, P. C. Ducorron, R. G. Davis, J. W. E. Maikai, Makalena, Kanihina, D. P. Mahoe, Mahelona, I. Kawa, Kalauhala, W. C. Parke, H. S. Swinton, Jno. E. Barnard.

Mr. Montgomery then moved that a committee of three be appointed to prepare and submit resolutions to the meeting. The following persons were appointed by the Chair for that purpose:—Mr. Montgomery, Mr. J. P. Griswold and Mr. R. G. Davis.

Mr. Montgomery, upon the return of the Committee to the room, read the following resolutions, which were moved and seconded, and unanimously adopted:

Whereas, It has pleased Almighty God, by an inscrutable decree of His providence, to remove from our midst the Honorable William L. Lee, Chief Justice of the Supreme Court of this Kingdom, who, during a period of eleven years, by his urbanity of manner, kindness of heart, and integrity of character, had endeared himself to us all; now, therefore, be it

Resolved, That we, as members of the Bar and officers of the Court over which he so long presided, deeply deplore the blow which has fallen upon us; and while we bow with submission and reverence before the will of Omniscient Power, experience a heartfelt sorrow that one so long our chief, and so eminently fitted for the position he occupied, should be taken away in the prime of his manhood.

Resolved, That as a mark of respect for his memory, and an expression of our feelings, the usual badge of mourning be worn by the members of the Bar and officers of the Supreme Court for the period of sixty days, and that in a body we attend his funeral.

Resolved, That the District Attorney of Oahu be requested to present to the Supreme Court, at the next term thereof, the proceedings of this meeting, and request on behalf of the Bar that they be entered of record.

Resolved, That we deeply and sincerely sympathize with the relatives and friends of the departed, and above all with his bereaved wife; and that the Secretary of this meeting be requested to forward to Mrs. Lee a copy of these resolutions, as a testimonial of our feelings towards her, and to cause the same to be published.

ASHER B. BATES, Chairman.

J. E. Barnard, Secretary.

Honolulu, 20th May, 1857.

At a meeting of the Officers and Directors of the American Club of Honolulu, called at the rooms of the Club, on Friday, May 29th, on occasion of the decease of the Honorable Wm. L. Lee, the following resolutions were unanimously adopted:

Resolved, That we have heard with deep regret of the death of our fellow countryman, Wm. L. Lee, Chief Justice of the Supreme Court of the Hawaiian Islands, and that in his death the nation has lost one of its most useful and valuable officers, whose character and integrity had gained for him the highest respect both at home and abroad; this Club has lost one of its founders, a most efficient member, and one whom we all were proud to claim as countryman and friend.

Resolved, That we tender to the bereaved widow of our deceased friend our our heartfelt sympathies in the affliction which she has been called by an all-wise Providence to endure:

That an invitation be extended to the American residents of Honolulu to assemble at the Rooms of the Club at three o'clock P. M. on Sunday next, for the purpose of attending the funeral and paying the last sad tribute to the remains of the deceased:

That the members of this Club wear the usual badge of mourning for thirty days:

That a copy of these Resolutions be presented by the Secretary to the widow:

That the Secretary be instructed to publish the foregoing Resolutions in the journals of this city, and to enter them on the Records of the Club.

Per order. ALEX. J. CARTWRIGHT, Secretary.

Lahaina, Maui, June 1st, 1857.

Early on Saturday morning last, the *Favorite* brought to this place intelligence of the decease of the Hon. William L. Lee. Although of late little or no hopes were entertained of his recovery, yet the announcement of his death was received in this community with feelings of unmingled sorrow. All classes of men seemed to feel that a good, a tried and trusty public servant, had passed away, never to return. At three o'clock in the afternoon of the same day, a meeting of the government officers, members of the Bar, and residents generally was convened at the Court House, when on motion of P. H. Treadway, Esq., the Hon. Edward P. Bond was chosen chairman, and Mr. J. C. Farwell, Secretary. Upon taking the Chair Mr. Bond alluded briefly, but with much feeling, to the public and private virtues which adorned the character of the deceased. There was, he said, a purity, beauty and simplicity in his life, that endeared him to all who were honored with his friendship; and that to his learning and labors we owe, in a great measure, the simplicity, system and comparative completeness of our judiciary.

The meeting was also addressed by Rev. S. E. Bishop, and G. D. Gilman, Esq., both of whom, in language simple and expressive, testified their high appreciation of the exalted character of the deceased, and the loss the nation is called upon to mourn in his death.

A Committee of three, consisting of Messrs. Farwell, Treadway and Gilman, was then appointed to draw up resolutions to be submitted at an adjourned meeting to be held on Monday next, at nine o'clock. Accordingly at the appointed hour this morning, there was a large attendance, embracing nearly all the foreign residents of Lahaina, when Mr. Farwell, on behalf of the committee, read the following resolutions which were adopted:

Resolved, That the intelligence of the death of the Hon. William L. Lee, Chief Justice of the Supreme Court of this kingdom, has created in this community feelings of deep and unaffected regret, that one so pure in life, so gifted and so generally esteemed for his public and private virtues, should be called away in the prime of manhood, and at a time when the nation can so ill afford the loss of his sound judgment, legal erudition, and temperate counsels.

Resolved, That for the character of the deceased as a jurist and a Christian gentleman, this community has ever entertained feelings of mingled admiration and respect.

Resolved, That this community would respectfully tender to His Majesty their sincere condolence at the loss he has sustained in the death of him who in life labored so earnestly to elevate the dignity of the kingdom, and promote the welfare of its people.

Resolved, That this community tender to the heads of His Majesty's Government their sympathy in the loss of a colleague whose reputation, as head of the Judiciary Department, was not confined to the kingdom alone, but was acknowledged with confidence and approbation by the representatives of every civilized country in comity with this.

Resolved, That, recognising as this community does, the sacred character of the grief of her who mourns a bereavement so far greater even than our own, it is with reluctant diffidence that we approach to offer to her our heartfelt sympathy and testimony to the virtues and amenities that have rendered her departed husband so generally respected and beloved while among us.

Resolved, That the Secretary of this meeting be instructed to forward a copy of these Resolutions to His Majesty, and to the widow of the deceased, and that he also furnish copies to the *Polynesian* and *Commercial Advertiser* newspapers for publication.

J. C. FARWELL, Secretary.

www.ingramcontent.com/pod-product-compliance
Lightning Source LLC
LaVergne TN
LVHW011142110826
845150LV00008B/2474
* 9 7 8 1 4 1 8 1 9 2 6 8 6 *